What I Wish I Said To You

By Isaac Paredes

To all of the people still going through a rough patch,
I promise life gets better.

Grief is in two parts. The first is loss. The second is the remaking of life.

Anne Roiphe

Preface

There are quite a few things in life that can push each of us to the edge. Whether the loss of a loved one or the moments when life just isn't going our way, we can often forget the beauty and wonderment that is and can be life. This book is proof that someone can reach the depths of their soul and still come back hopeful for brighter days.
Don't lose hope.

It's on nights like these
Where I look to the stars to find my peace

Millions of lights just shining bright
Even though most of them have already died

It's on nights like these
Where I feel like I'm completely at ease
Knowing there's no one left to hurt me
But inside

It's...poetic almost...
Just like the stars,
people have left, but I still see them
In my scars

Just like the stars
My loved ones are around me
But feel so far

Then there's you

Your smile, those mahogany eyes
The look to make me forget the lies

I'm sorry...I forget myself sometimes

I know you wouldn't mind
Cause my head doesn't always work right
But your head works just like mine

Am I allowed to say you're beautiful?
When those umber eyes gaze to the distant lands of better days

Am I allowed to say you're gorgeous
In the sad way you make eye contact and look away?

Am I allowed to admire your humor
With every wise remark and farce you make?

Am I allowed to notice the small things
The things that make you this way

If I was allowed to
I'd tell you every day

That your mind is perfect imperfection

Your heart rivals the beat of a summer rainstorm

Those eyes could swallow black holes
In the way they siphon my words away

That smile... has the power to change night to day...

But till then, I keep my mind locked away
My heart, trapped in a cage
For the hope that one day
I'm allowed to say your name

To think you're teaching me to be in the moment

How to enjoy the ticking seconds
Blowing by with every breath

Showing me how to be more open
To the many people in my path
And the days I have left

Showing me how to be happy
With me, the world, reality
Through the pain, murder, and theft

Teaching me how to love
To be unconditional and forthright

Showing me the reason we met

The world around me, fading
My words failing
As I think of you

I'm not sure what to say
Or how to say the truth

Deep down inside
I so truly am in love with you

But my words falter
As I fall into my ways

Drunk in love
Blame my mother and father
Oh no, I'm not enough for you to stay

But you do…

You always do anyways

Maybe you think I'm better,
That past the yelling and anger,
You see my tears and fears too

Maybe you know
I'm most afraid of losing you

Dopamine, serotonin, oxytocin
Just to name a few

Norepinephrine, vasopressin
All because of you.

Give me a biology lesson
As I look into those eyes
There's a science to it all,
It just took me by surprise.

The data speaks for itself
But what of attraction?
Love or Lust?

It's hard not to think about
But my thoughts are the only thing I trust

My heart is trapped in the deep blue sea
The science has my head in the clouds
Especially when you make it a reality
I wish I knew how to fight the doubt

It's not your fault.

Promised the world and its riches,
Love,
And all the sunlight reaches

It's not your fault
That you were left shattered
Into thousands of beautiful pieces
Each, watching on as you pick them up alone...

It's not your fault
For thinking you're not enough
But take a moment to look in the mirror
And see the angel from up above

See the smile that makes the earth spin
The heart that makes my world glisten

See the girl who deserves it all
But wants nothing more
Then love and someone to call

I'll cut my hands with you picking up the pieces
Reforming that heart
Remaking the creases
Gently holding those velvet soft hands
Until you see the beautiful angel I see

Until you realize you're more than enough for me...

Talk to me and show me the world in your eyes
Show me the beauty, monochrome, loneliness inside

Show me the heart too battered to try

Give me a chance to show you mine

Cause we have the same mess in our minds
Similar scars, stories, feelings to hide
Like two floating puzzle pieces that finally collide
Something tells me that one day, we could shine

But please, dear, take your time
There's no rush, we have until the stars align

You are

The diamond in the rough
Food on the lonely island
Freshwater in the middle of the sea
A miracle when people find it hard to believe,

You are the blood to the heart
The oxygen to the air

You are the perfect reflection

Modern Art

Silk too pure to tear

So take my hand through the next door
I'll gladly break my heart
To fix yours

Is it the fire behind those hidden eyes
Or the sound of your laughter and breath?

Maybe the fairness of your skin
The beauty within
There isn't much of my heart left

So take my hand
And my mind instead

Show me what love is
Make the world new and the sun dim
Show me what it's like to love again

In return, I'll lend you my future

The blossoming rose making time blur

In winter and summer, the flame will always burn
Cause deep down inside
It was always you to return

Take one step
And see the glimmering violet
Of the night sky

Take my hand, dear
Hang on tight

Lose yourself when I'm here

The grass sways with your breath
The lights reflect your eyes

And rain, your heart
Beating to the sound of a million cars

Thousands of fireflies
Fill the air
But one catches your eye

My fingers slip and you're gone

The night, darker than most

Left alone

With the moon to keep me company

The chances seem to escape me
Like fireflies from a jar
Flittering their steady wings
While I watch heartbroken from afar

Life has a funny way to tell us, "not yet"

Waiting through the cold on long winter nights
To boiling summer days

You'd wonder why I'd want to throw it all away

But I wouldn't, not after all I've bled
Cause deep down we all know
Something's gotta give
I just don't know what yet...

I want to write you
But a part of me just can't write anymore

Constantly barking up the same tree
I'm slowly growing tired of being me

Of seeing the world in monochrome
While everyone bathes in newly found colors

I'm
Slightly tired of trying to talk
To people too selfish to want
Anything else in life but meaningless sex
Faltering minutes of arrogant attempts
To feel better than others

And on the off chance
They feel fine and free their minds
They break bones to follow the broken home
They once left behind

Maybe it's the tree

Maybe it's me

Or maybe the world is too full of people
Too tired to dream

Where the sky meets the earth
A soliloquy forms
A quiet quivering attempt
At matching the mood
As you are the sun
And I am the moon

You make me shine

Don't leave too soon…

You reflect warmth, danger, and life
I become cold and dark when I'm not in your light
I'd become invisible each and every night
But I guess I'll be fine…

Love feels like the one thing I cannot get

That's the one thing that seems to tease me
Seems to always be just out of my grasp
Love

The reason I keep going
The reason I keep trying
The reason for my bleeding
Love
What makes this pain worthwhile
What gives me hope and breaks me all the same
Fuck…

Let me be real.
Let me think straight.
The tears have a way of blinding from the truth,
From reality.

What did I want?
What did you take?

What did you see in me?
Why did you let me believe?
No, no more words.

Hide the lies
The truths
The pain
The stains
The scars
Hideaway.

Looking up to the stars, the beautiful lights
They make for bearable nights
They show me a future where I can smile bright
Not alone, awaken to the morning light
Gosh...what a sight…
but not today.
Not tonight.

What can I say other than it's okay?
Maybe my world is collapsing

The death of one or pain of another

Maybe balls of fire are spiraling down
As the sirens wail for naught

"Get to safety, get to safety"

But for what?

When my walls are tumbling
And heaven is burning down
When hell opens up
And it's you and I left on the ground

Maybe we can share a smile and dance
Cause for once in our lives
We don't need to stand

It'd be okay to just live in the moment
As time stands still
Hand in hand, we lose our minds and say
It's finally okay

Looking in the mirror
Seeing what you're missing

Turning away

Thinking you weren't enough
Thinking you weren't in love
And hoping
You'll see what you never did those days

That he is what you never could be

Hoping
She's finally happy

When deep down you know
Without her,
You never will be

You are your own enemy.
Take a moment and look around
See the faces that surround you.
Look at the smiles and laughs
The eyes too drunk to keep track
Of the time that's slipping away.
No one hates you like you do
And no one cares enough to
Cause at the end of the day
It's always the same
When your demons decide to stay

The world doesn't need fixing
You do
Cause the whole can't fix
Without the parts too

So take a moment and hug the ones you love
Find a reason to take a break from the run

Face the demons hanging around
Make a few friends, learn to not drown.

Take it from someone who's felt the dark
Dropped in a void, made my own spark

Take it from someone on the outside

You never know how lucky you are
Until time says goodbye

What kind of world is this
Where to love is to conquer

Is that what it means to be human?

You cry
You hate the skin you're in
Too scared to look in the mirror
As you burn your lungs away

Yeah, smile all you can.
For making that smile flip
For switching courage with fear
And for leaving a mark of pain to stain
A heart so beautiful.

Smile all you can
Because at the end of this,
She won't remember you.
She'll look in the mirror and smile again.

Yeah, smile all you can
Because *she* lost out on a beautiful soul
And tried to corrupt it.

Smile all you fucking can
Because at the end of this,
She'll be long gone
With every step and mile
Finding new reasons to smile.

My phone is at 8%
It's 1 am, I'm still in bed
But the words scare me
7%
I'm in my head
Not yours instead
6%
And the clock is winding down
Soon I'll be in darkness
Silence to drown in
5%
And you're still reading this
Surprised you stood so long
Maybe if you came sooner
All of this pain would be gone
4%
And all I get
Is the chance to ask you one question

What was it that broke inside of you?
That sent you off searching
Down empty avenues?

Rooms, cold and smoky
But you stumble through
Looking for a little truth, somehow

What was it inside you that love never satisfied?
The thin thread that held you,
How did it come untied?

The grace you only ran from
The bridges that you burned
The peace of mind you learned to live without
The burdens of the people you've hurt

And all of your mistakes
You're looking for a place to hide them away

Did you find it now?

Like turning to a new chapter

I'd like to know before my phone dies
Cause I'll follow soon after

A Message to the reader

Thank you for reading my work and I truly hope you enjoyed the
time you spent reading it.
I would like to take this chance to invite you to reach out to your
loved ones if you are going through anything.
If you have no one to vent to, please feel free to reach out to me
@Numberspoetry on Instagram.

Be safe and be well.
Brighter days are on the way!

Acknowledgments

Thank you to my family for always pushing me to be a better person.
Thank you, Felix and Yianni for keeping me sane through the process of writing this book.

Made in the USA
Coppell, TX
27 August 2022

82168229R00015